What they don't

VIKINGS

By Bob Fowke

Dedicated to Egil Skallagrimsson,
a writer who knew how to handle a sword.

*Hodder
Children's
Books*

a division of Hodder Headline plc

Hallo, my name's *Bjorn the Blood-Crazy*. Pay attention or I'll slice your head from your shoulders with one blow of my trusty battleaxe. You're about to join me and my *venomous* Viking pals on a really *bloody* adventure. So get ready, I'll make sure you *bite into* all the really *gory bits*.

Text and illustrations, copyright © Bob Fowke 1996

The right of Bob Fowke to be identified as the author and artist of the work has been asserted by him in accordance with the Copyright, Designs and Patents Act 1988.

Produced by Fowke & Co. for Hodder Children's Books

Cover portrait of the Grandsons of Gostosmysl: Rurick, Truvori and Sineus by I Glazunov from the Russian Museum, St. Petersburg, courtesy of the Bridgeman Art Library, London, BAL 40951.

Published by Hodder Children's Books 1996

10 9 8 7 6 5 4 3

ISBN 0340 68611 1

Hodder Children's Books

a Division of Hodder Headline plc

338 Euston Road

London NW1 3BH

Printed and bound by The Guernsey Press Co. Ltd., Guernsey, Channel Islands

A Catalogue record for this book is available from the British Library

WHAT'S IN THIS BOOK

👣 Watch out for the *Sign of the Foot*! Whenever you see this sign in the book it means there are some more details at the *FOOT* of the page. Like here.

Keep your eyes open for the *Blood-splat Spot!* When the blood-splat splats beside a name this means there are more details in the *Villainous Vikings Hall of Fame* on page 123.

First of all, let's find out how everything started.

SMASH AND GRAB!

THEY CAME, THEY SAW, THEY TOOK

It's early morning on the 8th June AD 793. A tired grumpy monk wipes his bleary eyes - never a decent night's sleep when you have to go to church in the middle of every night. And this year his sleep has been ruined by freak whirlwinds and extra powerful lightning. There has even been talk of dragons flying in the air, although he hasn't seen any.

And now it's time for church again.

He glances out of the narrow window of his tiny cell. The sea looks grey and wild beneath a stormy sky. His monastery is Saint Aidan's

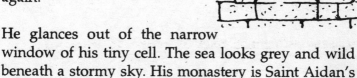

Monks had to go to church every three hours every day of the year. The names of the church services were: Matins, Laud, Prime, Terce, Sext, None, Vespers and Compline.

5

of Lindisfarne, a small island known as Holy Island, off the coast of Northumberland. All traffic between the monastery and the mainland is by a four-kilometre causeway which is underwater at high tide.

Lindisfarne is not an easy place to run away from.

Gazing wistfully out to sea, he sees some small dark specks bobbing far out on the water. Surely they can't be ships, there are too many of them? He looks more

WELL HALLO

carefully; they're ships all right, and an unusual shape. They curve upwards at the ends and look like dragons' heads. He blinks. Oh no, now he's seeing dragons too - that's what lack of sleep can do to you.

That's almost the only warning that Western Europe got of the Vikings. They appeared out of the blue and fell on Lindisfarne on that June day in AD 793 like a pack of blood-crazed hyenas. Here's how the attack was described by another monk, called Simeon, who lived in Durham three hundred years later:

Aaargh!

..the heathens  from the northern regions came with a fleet of ships to Britain. They came to the church of Lindisfarne, laid everything waste with grievous plundering, trampled the holy places with polluted steps, dug up the altars and seized all the treasures of the holy church. They killed some of the monks, took some away with them in fetters, many they drove out naked and loaded with insults, some they drowned in the sea.

Heathen meant people who weren't Christian, Jewish or Muslim. It comes from 'heath-dwellers' or wild people who lived on the heath.

Lindisfarne was the beginning of some of the bloodiest years in European history. Vikings found out that attacking monasteries was like ram-raiding without the risks. There was lots of treasure in monasteries and the monks weren't used to defending themselves.

But Vikings didn't stop at monasteries. The attack on Lindisfarne was the start of a reign of terror that went on for the next two hundred years ...

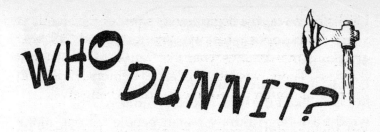

WHO DUNNIT?

INTRODUCING MR AND MRS VIKING

When the raid was over, the raiders of Lindisfarne escaped out to sea with their slaves and booty and headed north across the wild North Sea. They came from what is now called Scandinavia.

THE VIKING AGE LASTED FROM AD 800 TO 1100

ARCTIC CIRCLE

NORWAY

THIS WAY TO SANTA'S GROTTO

SWEDEN

DENMARK

SCANDINAVIA IS MADE UP OF NORWAY, SWEDEN AND DENMARK

BRITAIN WAS SPECIALLY VULNERABLE TO VIKING ATTACK BECAUSE IT HAD SUCH A LONG COAST LINE.

SITE OF WHITEHART LANE FOOTBALL GROUND

LOVELY AND HOT DOWN HERE

> We looked pretty good, though I say so myself.

HIM

People were scared stiff of Vikings, but they liked the look of these 'ruthless wrathful foreign purely pagan people' as one monk described them. This is what a Viking chief looked like in *Njall's Saga* , written in Iceland:

- ANGRY EYES
- SILK HEADBAND
- MAKE-UP - WELL SOMETIMES
- LONG HAIR
- WELL KEPT BEARD AND MOUSTACHE
- AXE
- HELMET
- BLUE TUNIC
- SILVER BELT
- BLUE STRIPED TROUSERS
- ROUND SHIELD
- BLACK BOOTS

A saga was a Viking *story*, but not a *poem* - remember that.

10

HER

Before they became Christian, pagan 🐾 Vikings could have more than one wife plus several concubines 🐾. Viking women were known for their independent ways. The top wife of a Viking was seen as almost the equal of her husband. She showed this by hanging her keys from a brooch on her chest.

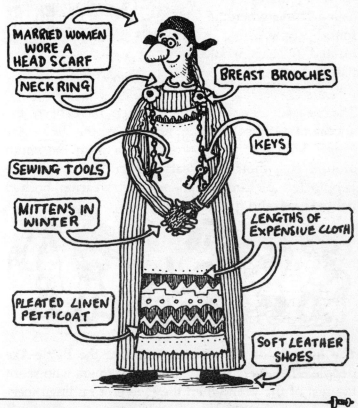

MARRIED WOMEN WORE A HEAD SCARF

NECK RING

BREAST BROOCHES

KEYS

SEWING TOOLS

MITTENS IN WINTER

LENGTHS OF EXPENSIVE CLOTH

PLEATED LINEN PETTICOAT

SOFT LEATHER SHOES

🐾 A pagan is like a heathen. In this book it means people who worshipped the old Viking gods.

🐾 Concubines were women who lived with a man but were not married.

A BIT OF BACKGROUND

The very first account of Scandinavia is by an ancient Greek called Pytheas who sailed from Marseilles in the south of France around 330 BC, looking for a sea route to the tin and amber trade of Northern Europe. He sailed up the coast of Norway to a land called Thule, where he found people who hunted for seals, whales, fish and seagulls.

Seagull

The people seen by Pytheas must have been the ancestors of the Vikings, known as the *Battle-Axe People*, who arrived in Scandinavia from the south around two thousand years earlier. The Battle-Axe People left pictures of themselves wearing horned helmets ⚔ and fighting with axes.

The lifestyle of the Vikings was like the Battle-Axe people. They were mostly off-duty farmers who spent the rest of the year, when they weren't raiding, knee-

 Their Viking descendants did not wear horns on their helmets. Horns are not very practical when fighting. They can catch a sword-blow and are easy to grab hold of.

deep in cow-muck or minding their sheep on the Scandinavian hillsides. Here's a typical farm:

THE GRABBIT HABIT

No one knows for sure why the Vikings got in the habit of raiding. Perhaps it was a mixture of reasons:

Be that as it may, they certainly liked ships - the word *Viking* seems to have come from an old word 'vik' meaning a bay or creek. In fact the Vikings usually described themselves by the area they came from ...

Other people called them Norsemen, Danes or Rus, as well as a lot of names which are too rude to print!

How Did They Get Away With It?

The reason a bunch of off-duty farmers from a freezing cold land in the far north could smash up the rest of Europe was because Europe was going through a bad patch at the time ...

EUROPE IN AD 814

VIKINGS COULD RAID FAR INLAND UP RIVERS

EMPEROR CHARLEMAGNE DIED IN 814. HIS EMPIRE DIVIDED.

HUNS INVADED EUROPE FROM THE EAST ON HORSEBACK.

SARACENS, OR ARABS, INVADED FROM THE SOUTH.

The Huns later settled down in what is now Hungary.

14

MONK STORY

As the monks of Lindisfarne had found out, it was a specially bad time to be a monk because monasteries were full of treasure. Take the monks of St. Philibert, in France:

600 Monastery on the island of Noirmoutier on the river Loire.

862 Monks move inland to Poitou to escape Viking raids.

872-3 Monks move further inland to Moulins.

875 They move to Tournus, still trying to escape Viking raids; they had fled 965 km in 13 years.

937 Raided again - by Huns from the east!

SEARCHING FOR CLUES

The Vikings lived at a time of war and barbarian invasion. Not many people were writing books so we don't know much about them. In fact so little remains that investigating them is like trying to solve some complicated puzzle with half the bits missing. Fortunately the Vikings left a handful of clues behind:

CLUE NO 1 - THE DAYS OF THE WEEK

The gods of the old English and the Vikings were very similar. Some of our weekdays are named after the same gods as the Viking gods. Viking gods were fierce and quarrelsome - like the people.

TUESDAY

The sky god and god of war was called Tyr in Scandinavia and Tiw in England. Prisoners of war may have been sacrificed to him. Tuesday is named after him.

WEDNESDAY

The top god was called Woden in England and Odin by the Vikings. Wednesday (Woden's Day) is his day. More about him later.

Thor was the god of thunder, among other things. He was a vast red-haired man with a red beard and red eyebrows. He carried a hammer called Mjolnir and had a pair of iron gauntlets. When he rode across the sky in his chariot drawn by two sacred goats the thunder rumbled and crashed. Thursday is named after him.

Frigg or Freyya was the goddess of love and the home. She had lots of arguments with her husband, Odin, which she often won. Friday is her day.

CLUE NO 2 - PLACE NAMES

Some Vikings stayed on after the raiding season was over. In several countries they settled in large numbers and mixed with the local people. We can tell where they settled by looking at the names of towns and villages. In north-west England there are hundreds of places ending in '-by', such as Weatherby; 'by' was Viking for a small village or farm.

CLUE NO 3 - BURIED TREASURE

A lot of clues about the Vikings have been found underground. Several rich 'hoards' have been found of objects beautifully made of gold, silver and iron. Archaeologists have also found out a lot about how the Vikings lived from everyday objects which may not be treasure but can be even more interesting.

CLUE NO No 4 - RUNES

The Vikings had their own alphabet called Runic. They carved messages on wayside stones and in other places such as bridges. Some historians can read the messages.

CLUE NO 5 - SAGAS AND POEMS

Sagas and poems were normally about exciting adventures, heroes and myths. Poems were remembered and spoken aloud at first. Later some of them were written down.

CLUE NO 6 - THE ANGLO-SAXON CHRONICLE

The Saxons lived in England during the Viking period. They kept a record of everything important which happened each year. The Anglo-Saxon Chronicle describes many Viking attacks (see page 94).

 Archaeologists are historians who specialise in digging up remains from the past.

COULD **YOU** HAVE DUNNIT?

Check it out - are you bad Viking material? (part 1)

I WHICH TOY DO YOU LIKE BEST?

a A doll

b A blood-stained axe

c A model boat

2 WHICH IS RIGHT?

a Friday was once the traditional day for human sacrifice by frying the victims.

b Friday was once a free-day or holiday.

c Friday is named after a goddess called *Frigg* or *Freyya*.

3 WHICH GAME DO YOU LIKE BEST?

a Mummies and Daddies

b Fighting

c Football

Answers on page 122.

19

HOME SWEET HOME

WE'RE JUST FARMERS!

Scandinavia is freezing cold for a lot of the year especially in the far north. The first Viking raiders of Britain probably came from Norway, where remote scattered farms still cling to the steep hills as they sweep down towards the icy fjords below. (In the south the farms were clustered together in villages). Life was tough for the small-time farmers who made up the backbone of Viking raiding parties.

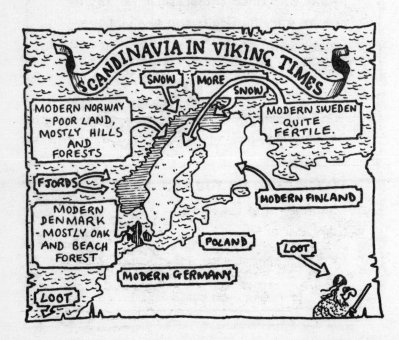

SCANDINAVIA IN VIKING TIMES

SNOW   MORE SNOW

MODERN NORWAY - POOR LAND, MOSTLY HILLS AND FORESTS

MODERN SWEDEN - QUITE FERTILE.

FJORDS

MODERN FINLAND

MODERN DENMARK - MOSTLY OAK AND BEACH FOREST

POLAND

LOOT

MODERN GERMANY

LOOT

GETTING THERE

It was hard to travel from one farm to another on the muddy tracks and there were no bridges anywhere as far as we know. So winter, when the mud was frozen, was the easiest time to get around. When the snow came a Viking on the move would wrap up warm against the bitter cold before strapping on a pair of skis, skates or snow-shoes, all of which were invented by the ancestors of the Vikings.

Skis were good for sport as well as travel.

Skates were made of bone, and skaters would push themselves around on the ice with spoked sticks.

They also had sledges and would fit iron spikes onto horses' hooves so that they could get a better grip on the ice.

HOME AT LAST!

At night in the far north the cold can freeze your eyeballs and worse ✎ , so the houses for both people and animals have to be extra warm. When they settled in Greenland near the Arctic Circle the Vikings built cowsheds like castles against the cold, with turf walls nearly two metres thick and with a great mound of turf piled on top for a roof. The entrances were long narrow passages to keep out as much cold air as possible.

A typical Viking liked his house to be long - very long. Usually there was one enormous room with walls which curved inwards at the ends, a reminder of earlier times when upturned boats were used as roofs. Their longhouses might be made out of wood or stones or even entirely out of turf like the Greenland cowsheds. In turf houses, dry wood panels were built inside, standing free of the damp turf walls.

People ate and slept on wide earth platforms which ran down both sides of a longhouse. The low rough gulley between them was used for cooking and for a fire, and probably for leaving muddy boots. There was no chimney; the stench of smoke, food, animals and unwashed bodies must have been enough to make a skunk vomit.

When people suffer from frost-bite the frozen bits, usually fingers and toes but sometimes the nose and ears, go black and then fall off.

BEST SEATS IN THE HOUSE BETWEEN THE CARVED COLUMNS.

FOUR CENTRE COLUMNS WERE SPECIALLY CARVED

OIL LAMP

DOUBLE ROW OF COLUMNS

BEDDING

RAISED PLATFORM OF FLATTENED EARTH.

HEARTH

USEFUL CHEST

PEOPLE SMELLS

SMALL LOW TABLES

ANIMAL SMELLS

GRUB'S UP

Apart from big feasts which were a favourite Viking hobby, there were two main meals a day, one in the morning after everyone had been working for a couple of hours, and the other in the evening. Some Viking dishes are still eaten today. Blood soup, known as *svartsoppa* was a great favourite in the autumn when the pigs were slaughtered and is still popular. No doubt Vikings ate an early version of *smorgasbord*, which meant 'smear fatty goose table' but is now a collection of cold meats and cheeses.

People slurped up their blood soup and other tasty morsels with spoons made out of wood or deer's antler. They used wooden bowls and flat wooden trenchers, which are like a sort of plate.

Vikings who settled in Iceland hardly ate any greens, just a few leeks and a bit of seaweed.

A Hunting We Will Go

Most Vikings liked to hunt. In the far north hunting was vital for survival.

Tasty Morsels

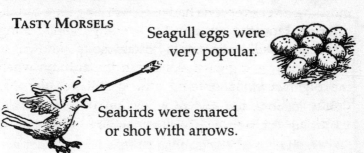

Seagull eggs were very popular.

Seabirds were snared or shot with arrows.

For That Extra Something

Furs, hides, whalebone, walrus tusks, live falcons and feathers were all traded for luxuries from further south.

A Substantial Meal

Bear, wild boar, elk and reindeer were all hunted and eaten. Seals were speared or netted, while whales were harpooned from small boats then towed ashore.

AH, DINNER!

The farming life could be tough and boring. Raiding was much more fun.

DEAR DIARY
A Year in the Life of Harald Homebody

Six Winter Months
Stay indoors, too cold to go out apart from a little hunting and fighting. Shall get on with some indoor work, and if that's too boring, there's always feasting.

April (Cuckoo Month)
Time to put the boots on, must start ploughing. The slaves can do a bit of peat-digging and wood-cutting for next winter's fire. Oh, and they'll have to repair the walls round the fields and make sure they're well-manured with dung. My son, Thorkil, is due to set off on a raiding expedition this month. I don't think I'll go with him - still got a bit of trouble with the sword wound I collected in Northumbria last August.

May - June (Lambs'-Fold Time)
Must send the slaves and children to gather seabirds' eggs from the cliffs. I shall get on with the lamb-weaning and later the sheep-shearing. Also I must go and defend myself at the local *Thing* ◀ . Someone says that I killed their son last winter - well I was drunk and he called me a pig. What's wrong with being drunk?

Thing was the Viking word for an assembly. It was a cross between a local law court and a parliament.

June - July
Drive the cattle and sheep to the high pastures, the slaves can stay with them.

July - August (Hay-Making Month)
All hands to the scythe! Women and children as well as free men and slaves. Must collect as much hay as possible, not just from the fields, but from the open countryside. Then it's time to start harvesting the cereal crops such as oats and rye - I'm exhausted!

September - October
Round up the animals from the mountain pastures and sort them out by their ear-marks. Some must be slaughtered and the meat dried or salted to stop it going bad. Lots of lovely pig's blood to eat during the slaughter - yum!

Winter again
Must break down the walls round the cornfields so that the cattle can get to the stubble. Thorkil's back safe and sound and he's brought lots of treasure. Beginning of winter is a good time for feasts, as we've still got plenty of fresh food, and not too much work to do.

> The scruffy English said we had an unfair advantage with the local girls because we bathed once a week, combed our hair and changed our underwear.

SAVAGE SAUNAS

After a hard day's hunting or farming there was nothing a Viking liked better than a good hot bath, although often he had to wait for Saturday, which was bathday. Bath houses were built separately from the main farm and were a bit like steam baths or saunas. Water was thrown on to a pile of red-hot stones to make the steam. For those who liked to get really hot there was a shelf which ran round the walls high up. A Viking could lie there and swelter until he was red as a beetroot. When the bathers were all pink and rosy they might finish off by whipping themselves with bundles of twigs or even rolling in the snow.

TIME FOR BED

At the end of the evening the tables were cleared away and bedding was unrolled on the earth platforms. Important people might even have lockable wood-panelled bed cupboards.

NIGHT NIGHT

WILD WOMEN

- SO WATCH OUT!

There was no place for idle hands on a Viking farm. While Viking men were out fighting or farming, Viking women were busy from morning to night:

THINGS TO DO BY BUSY BRUNHILDE

HELP WITH THE HAY-MAKING AND HARVEST

DO THE COOKING, WITH THE HELP OF OTHER WOMEN AND THE SLAVES

WAAA!

DO THE SPINNING AND WEAVING

HAVE THE BABIES

RAISE THE CHILDREN

DO THE MILKING AND MAKE THE BUTTER AND CHEESE

ALSO - TREAT FAMILY AND WORKERS WHEN THEY ARE SICK. MAYBE DO A BIT OF FORTUNE-TELLING. GET TIRED AND SLEEP

A young man who was interested in a girl had to be very careful. If he showed too much interest by paying her lots of visits or writing poems to her or other such soppy behaviour, and then he didn't marry her, her father might well take *blood vengeance*. If nothing else, the young man might end up paying money. One set of laws suggested the following fines if a man touched a woman whom he wasn't meant to touch:

SHOULDER (OR JUST ABOVE THE KNEE) - 47 GRAMS OF SILVER.

ELBOW (OR LEG BETWEEN KNEE OR CALF) - 75 GRAMS OF SILVER.

WRIST OR ANKLE - 113 GRAMS OF SILVER.

The A to D of Getting Married

ADORATION
It helped if a girl and a boy liked each other.

BETROTHAL
If the families of the girl and boy were agreeable there would be a betrothal meeting where the *bride-price* was fixed. This was money paid by the husband to the wife's family, which had to be repaid if there was a divorce later. If no bride-price was paid then the wife would be just a concubine. In fact one way for a man to get a concubine was simply to capture her and cart her off.

CEREMONY
The marriage ceremony included drinking of 'bridal-ale' and a feast followed by going to bed together before witnesses. Women kept their own surnames.

DIVORCE
Divorce was easily arranged and could be asked for by husband or wife. The reason for a divorce could be quite a little thing such as a wife  wearing trousers or a husband wearing a girlish shirt.

Viking houses must have been swarming with all the children of the wives and concubines - although not quite as swarming as they could have been; sickly babies  were often left outside to die. It was not a crime to kill a baby before it had started to suck milk at the breast.

There was no such thing as a Viking school, and there was no place for a 'charcoal-chewer' - a child who lingered by the warmth of the hearth instead of working. Children were brought up tough, especially boys who were expected to like fighting. In fact it was almost a compliment to say that a little boy was quarrelsome or vengeful. Under twelve years of age, a specially quarrelsome boy could kill someone and not be punished, although his family had to pay compensation.

I ONLY KILLED HIM!

WELL THAT'S OKAY THEN.

Babies were 'baptised' by sprinkling water on them - this may have been a pagan custom before it was a Christian custom.

A Fistful of Fearsome Women

Some Viking women were peace-makers, but more often they are described in the sagas as fierce and proud. "Cold are women's counsels" said the Viking proverb.

Fredydis

Fredydis was the sister of the famous Viking, Leif Eriksson, who first explored the north-east coast of America. She travelled there with him on his second voyage. During their first winter in America she quarrelled with two brothers, Helgi and Finnbogi and then told her husband, a Greenlander called Thorvard, that the brothers had mistreated her. Fredydis persuaded her husband to attack the brothers. They were dragged from their house and murdered, together with their male followers, but this wasn't enough for Freydidis; she wanted the five women followers of the brothers killed as well. And since no one would kill them, Freydis took an axe and killed them herself.

The Red Girl

In the tenth century a fierce Viking woman, known as the Red Girl, was leader of a group of Vikings in Ireland.

VOLVA

Volva wasn't the name of an individual. A Volva was a female prophetess. Volvas would travel from farm to farm, sometimes in groups, and answer questions about the future. They were treated with great respect.

AUD THE DEEP-MINDED

Aud is not known to have killed anyone, but she was a very powerful woman. After the death of her husband, a Viking king in Ireland, she led her large family to the Orkney and Faroe Islands and then to Iceland where she gained control of vast lands.

GUTHRITH

Guthrith was the wife of Thorfinn Karlsefni, leader of the expedition to America which included Fredydis. While in America she gave birth to the first European ever to be born there, who was named Snorri  Thorfinnsson. She was a very clever woman who outlived her husband by several years after their return from America, and made a Christian pilgrimage to Rome. Having travelled between Rome, Greenland, Iceland, Norway and America she must have been one of the most widely-travelled people in the world up to that time.

WHAT DO YOU LIKE TO EAT?

Check it out - are you bad Viking material? (part 2)

1 FOR BREAKFAST?

a A bowl of cereal
b Wild seagulls' eggs
c A sliver of toast with
   marmalade

2 FOR LUNCH?

a Beer
b Lots of beer
c A low-calory
   salad sandwich

3 FOR SUPPER?
a boiled cabbage
b chocolate
c blood soup

Answers on page 122.

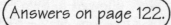

HAIRY KINGS, BALD SLAVES AND ER ... THING

WHO'S ON TOP - AND WHO ISN'T

POWER PEAR
Viking society was pear-shaped.

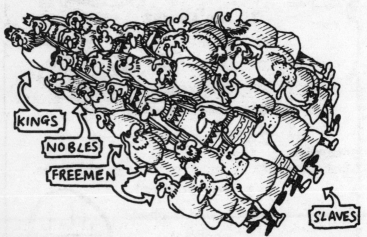

KINGS
NOBLES
FREEMEN
SLAVES

SCRUFFY SLAVES
At the bottom were the slaves. They had their hair shaved or close-cropped and wore simple white woollen clothes, but they were allowed to own property and might be given their freedom. Slaves had to watch out for the farmer's wife as well as the farmer: she ruled the roost within the walls of the farmhouse.

Slaves were thought to be stupid, dirty and cowardly.
It was specially shameful to be killed by a slave. One
poet gives them horrid names:

FREE MEN
Mostly farmers but could be craftsmen or traders.

AND LORDLY LORDS
At the top were the kings and powerful lords. The
centre of a king's or great lord's power was his hall,
which could be massive. Olaf the Peacock, descendant
of Aud the Deep-Minded, had a richly-carved hall
which could seat a thousand. Grouped around the
lord was his family and a group of trusted warriors,
called his *hird*, who received rich gifts and the booty of
Viking raids, and might be given land to farm. They

feasted with him during the long winter months and fought with him in all his battles.

Members of the hird who misbehaved had to sit in the lowliest positions in the hall. Everyone was allowed to throw animal bones at them for fun.

FEUD FRENZY

Whether grouped round a powerful lord or living on their own farm, Viking warriors had four big ideas:

What these four ideas added up to was *Feud Frenzy*. If anyone hurt your friend or your family you had to take revenge to save your honour, and that could start a quarrel or *blood-feud* between families which might go on for years. These feuds between families were common. There were enemies everywhere. Here's two Viking sayings for when you are going to a feast or you are out farming:

> *Before proceeding up the hall, study all the doorways.*
> *You never know when an enemy will be present.*
>
> *In the field no man should stir one step from where*
> *his weapons are.*

Friends and family were vital to help fight against so many enemies. To increase the size of their family, men sometimes swore blood-brotherhood, mixing their blood and earth together. From then on your blood-brother's enemy was your enemy, and your enemy was his enemy.

39

Feuds could end dramatically, for instance by a 'burning-in' when one party caught the other at home and burned the house down, so that people had to come out and be slaughtered or die in the flames. Or feuds might end if both parties were exhausted and agreed to accept blood-money instead of vengeance.

A neater way to sort out a quarrel was to agree to a duel:

1. Peg out a piece of cloth, around two metres square.

2. Dig three trenches round the cloth.

3. Place four hazel posts at the corners.

4. Take turns to strike each other.

5. Each fighter can have one friend who can protect his fighter with a shield (up to three shields can be used).

6. If blood is shed on the cloth, the wounded man can buy mercy.

7. Two feet beyond the hazel posts and you're said to be running away.

AT LAST ER ... THING

Quarrels were best settled at a court or *Thing*. These were assemblies of freemen which could be local or even national, like the Althing of Iceland. *Things* were a mixture of law court and parliament and mostly they were controlled by the local chiefs. When a decision was reached on a particular case, everyone clashed their weapons together to show their agreement.

Before you could take your case to a *Thing* you had to get there, and your enemies might try to ambush you on the way. It was important to gather as much support from friends and neighbours as possible before setting out. And when you got there it was best to remember that the law was more about keeping the peace than about justice. This is a Norwegian law:

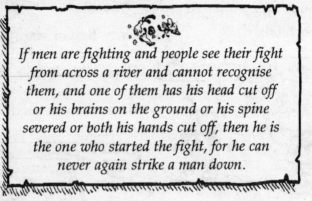

If men are fighting and people see their fight from across a river and cannot recognise them, and one of them has his head cut off or his brains on the ground or his spine severed or both his hands cut off, then he is the one who started the fight, for he can never again strike a man down.

Painful Punishments

If the *Thing* found you guilty there were three kinds of punishment:

1. Atonement

Every free person was classed by the amount of money they could expect to get for an injury done to them and by the amount they would have to pay if they injured someone else. Kings paid most, poor peasants paid the least.

The worse the injury, the greater the payment. The payment for a killing was called *mansbot*, but the victim's family could refuse to receive the payment and seek vengeance instead - which they tended to do, being Vikings.

2. PHYSICAL PUNISHMENT
Whipping and *mutilation* were strictly for slaves.

Hanging was for theft.

Beheading was a decent way to die for a free man.

Stoning

Stoning, drowning or *sinking in a bog* were for witchcraft.

Drowning

CLUB

Sinking

3. OUTLAWRY

As punishment for killing, a man might be declared an outlaw. This meant that he was literally outside the law. Anyone could kill him without fear of punishment, and his property went to the man who accused him. Actually it wasn't always that bad. The outlaw's friends and neighbours could protect him or he might be smuggled into exile abroad. Sometimes he was even allowed to live in a safe area near his home.

But there was never much doubt who the killer was, because if a killer had any sense he told everyone as soon as possible; a secret killing was the shameful crime of murder, while an open killing was only *man-slaying*, which was nothing to be ashamed about.

ARE YOU GUILTY - OR NOT GUILTY?

Check it out - are you bad Viking material? (part 3)

Imagine you are a Viking woman and you have been accused of adultery . You have sworn that you are innocent, but the *Thing* insists that you undergo *trial by ordeal* to prove your innocence. The Vikings probably learned trial by ordeal from Christians. The idea was that God would show whether the accused was innocent or guilty. After the ordeal your wound will be bandaged for several days and then you will be judged on how clean the wound is.

WHICH DO YOU CHOOSE?

a Pick up a bar of hot iron and walk nine paces before throwing it down.

b Pick stones from a pot of boiling water.

c Cross your heart and hope to die.

Answers on page 122.

Adultery is when a married person sleeps with someone other than their husband or wife.

DRUNK AS A SCANDINAVIAN SKUNK

TIME FOR BEER AND BALLADS

Feasting was a favourite Viking hobby. They did a lot of it. The best time to feast was the start of winter when there was plenty of food left from after the harvest and not much else to do. A good feast could go on for several days.

The host made sure his guests were met with water and a towel so that they could freshen up before the feast got under way. Food was served by the women. Sometimes the lord's wife and daughters would serve with their own hands, but when things got rowdy they might clear off - if there was another room to go to.

There was plenty of food of course, but there's no doubt that the most important thing at any feast was the drink. It was ladled into drinking horns from large buckets or bowls, and the thing about a drinking horn was that if you put it down it fell over, so it had to be emptied first. The result was that all the merry-makers got blind drunk, and because the drink was full of impurities they must have had the most horrific hangovers afterwards.

MORE!

MORE!

The next best thing to a feast or a fight was a good story told in a poem or a saga, and the good thing about stories was that Vikings could listen to them while they were feasting, thus enjoying two of their favourite hobbies at once. Poets were stars. The biggest star of all was Egil Skallagrimsson

LAGER SAGAS

There were two main types of poetry:
eddaic: fairly simple, all about legends and battles.
skaldic: more complicated, all about kings and battles.
Their poetry was littered with *kennings*. These were colourful names for things. For instance, the kenning for a ship might be *sea horse* or *wave-battler*. Kennings can make Viking poetry seem pretty weird. Try this short poem by the famous poet, Snorri Sturluson (answer upside down):

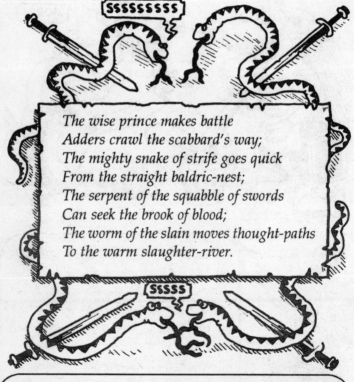

> The wise prince makes battle
> Adders crawl the scabbard's way;
> The mighty snake of strife goes quick
> From the straight baldric-nest;
> The serpent of the squabble of swords
> Can seek the brook of blood;
> The worm of the slain moves thought-paths
> To the warm slaughter-river.

Answer to poem - adders are swords, the snake of strife is a sword, the baldric-nest is its scabbard, the serpent of the squabble of swords is also a sword, as is worm of the slain, Thought-paths is the chest of an enemy, and the warm slaughter-river is lots of lovely blood for the sword to drink.

THINGS TO DO WHEN YOU'RE NOT DRUNK

When not feasting the lord and his men might play games:

Board games

A ball game played with a bat and hard ball. It could end in bloodshed.

Horse-fighting

Wrestling in water - drag your opponent under water and hold him there till he collapses.

LOONY RUNES

The Vikings had their own letters, called runes. Runes weren't much use for writing down long poems and sagas, but they were good for magic spells, and for memorials to the dead on stone and wood. They called the runic alphabet ◄ - the *futhark* after its first six letters.

This is the key to most popular version of the *futhark*. Using it, see if you can decode the loony rune below. There are clues in the picture to help you.

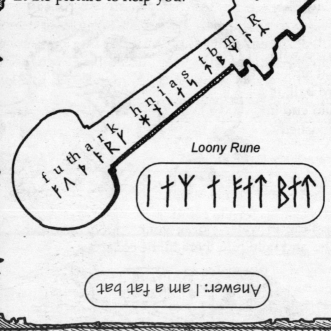

Loony Rune

Answer: I am a fat bat

Our word 'alphabet' comes from *alpha* and *beta*, the first two letters of the Greek alphabet.

WAR FEVER!

SUMMER HOLIDAYS VIKING-STYLE

The early Viking raids starting in 793 were small-scale affairs, like the first drops of rain before a storm. Local chieftains, mostly from Norway, would gather together a few warships and a small group of followers, perhaps less than a hundred. They would load up their ships with weapons, armour and food for the voyage, and set off in the spring or summer while the sea was fairly calm. It was best to get home before the winter weather set in, so they had to allow time for the return journey.

We launched the first raids from Norway, then from around AD 830 the Danes joined in, and the fun really started. The islands of Britain and Ireland took the brunt of our attacks. Vikings started staying on over winter and looking for land to settle down on. Read these scraps from my bloodstained scrap-book.

RAIDER'S DIGEST
The voice of Vikings everywhere
Circulation 2,000,000

SHERIFF SLASHED IN PORTLAND PUNCH UP 789

The crews of three Norwegian ships have killed the Sheriff of Dorset and all his men in the small town of Portland. The Sheriff ordered our boys to come with him to the royal palace - he should have known better!

LINDISFARNE LOOTERS LEAVE TRAIL OF BLOOD 793

Norwegian raiders have plundered the lonely abbey of Lindisfarne, off the Northumberland coast, in the first proper Viking raid on English soil. The success of the raid was due to smart planning and efficient execution of the plan, leading to loads of loot and slaves. Well done boys!

MONKS MISERABLE OVER PAGAN PRIESTESS 839

A Viking chieftain, Thorgisl, has set up his headquarters at Armagh in Northern Ireland. His excellent wife has started to make pagan prophecies from the altar of the local monastery. The monks have either left or been slaughtered.

EDITORIAL

That's enough complaints from the Irish about raids on their monasteries. It's well known that they are not above a spot of raiding themselves, especially when food is short. Irish monks can be as blood-thirsty as the common people. We remind our readers of the battle in 807 between the monasteries of Cork and Clonfert, which left mounds of dead monks and superiors.

DUBLIN NAMED 836

Congratulations to the first Viking settlers in Ireland who have founded their colony at a murky spot on the River Liffey. It's been named Dubb-Lin meaning Black Pool. The new town is expected to become a major base for the slave trade and for raiding into England.

DORESTADT DESTROYED BY DANISH DEVILS 834

The Vikings have opened their onslaught on the Frankish empire of mainland Europe with a devilishly devastating attack on the town of Dorestadt.

PARIS PLUNDERERS PAID PROTECTION MONEY 845

We understand that Charles the Bald, Emperor of the Franks, has paid 3,000 Kg of silver to a Viking army for them to leave Paris, in the first known payment of Danegeld in France.

DAMN IT THANET! 850

For the first time Danish Vikings have stayed over winter on the Isle of Thanet on the coast of Kent. This could be the start of a new trend for Vikings in England. We'll keep you posted.

GETTING TOOLED UP

There were laws saying what weapons a Viking had to take with him on a raid. In Sweden it was a shield, sword, spear and iron hat, and a mail coat or leather jerkin, a bow and a dozen arrows for each rowing bench of the ship.

THE COMPLETE VIKING

HELMET

'TWISTING SPEAR', PERHAPS THROWN WITH A CORD SO THAT IT ROTATED IN FLIGHT.

METAL SHIELD RIM—BUT NOT TOO HEAVY, THE SHIELD HAD TO BE QUITE LIGHT

IRON SHIELD BOSS FOR EXTRA KNUCKLE PROTECTION

CHAIN-MAIL SHIRT OR PADDED LEATHER JERKIN WHICH MIGHT HAVE PIECES OF BONE SEWN INTO IT.

ROUND SHIELD MADE OF THIN WOODEN BOARDS HELD TOGETHER BY AN IRON BAR ONE METRE ACROSS. LEATHER COVER PAINTED IN BRIGHT COLOURS

SWORD IN WOODEN SCABBARD LINED WITH OILED LEATHER OR WAXED CLOTH.

'BEARDED' AXE— WITH HOOK FOR GRAPPLING.

Swords were the favourite Viking weapon. They were given special names such as *Snake of Wounds* or *Leg-Biter* and were handed down from father to son. The best swords were made by pattern-welding. This made the steel extra hard by increasing the amount of carbon in the metal.

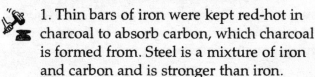

HOW TO PATTERN-WELD A SWORD

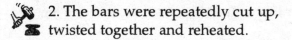

1. Thin bars of iron were kept red-hot in charcoal to absorb carbon, which charcoal is formed from. Steel is a mixture of iron and carbon and is stronger than iron.

2. The bars were repeatedly cut up, twisted together and reheated.

3. The red-hot, twisted bars were hammered together to make the central part of a swordblade.

4. Two red-hot strips of finest steel were hammered on to make the cutting edges.

5. The blade was 'quenched' to make it harder still. This meant plunging it into a cold liquid, perhaps honey or oil.

6. The edges were filed sharp and the blade polished by rubbing with vinegar or urine.

Swords weighed between one and two kilos and a skilful swordsman could fight with either hand, switching from left to right to confuse his enemy. For a Viking, skill with a sword counted for more than skill with a ball for a professional footballer today - it had to: his life depended on it.

SWORD TIPS FOR STARTERS

The important thing is to be strong and fast on your feet like a boxer, keep ducking and weaving, and take big leaps sideways and backwards to avoid having your legs slashed off.

Aim heavy slashing blows at your opponent's head or limbs. Try to hack off an arm or a leg.

Hold your shield well out from the body.
It's best to ward off blows with the flat of the shield and not with the iron rim. Your opponent may break his sword on the rim if you're lucky, but if he cuts through the rim he's pretty certain to split your shield in two.

Fight with the sun behind you, so that your opponent is blinded by the sun in his eyes.

Don't forget - in a formal duel you're allowed two more shields if the first gets broken.

GETTING STUCK IN

Battles started with a hail of arrows, spears or stones but soon broke up into a scrum of individual duels. One tactic was to form a *swine array* which meant marching forward in a wedge formation with the best men in the 'snout'. Another was to form a defensive 'shieldwall' if the battle was going against you. Later Vikings learned to use battering rams and catapults for attacking cities.

Most kings and leaders didn't live long. They fought at the front of a battle surrounded by trusty warriors, where the fighting was thickest.

Skilled fighters were highly-respected. One amazing skill was to catch a spear in mid-air with a back-hand stroke, swing right round in a circle and fling the spear back at your enemy, all in one movement.

Another trick was to throw a spear from each hand. The famous Viking king, Olaf Trygvasson 🐾, could do this.

One type of fighter was especially feared. This was the *berserker*. Berserk means bear-shirt. These were fighters dedicated to the god Odin, whose name meant furious or mad. They worked themselves up into a fighting madness by rhythmic howling and jumping (and possibly with drink) then fought naked in a *berserk rage*, not caring whether they lived or died. They were unstoppable in battle, but they were looked on with horror by normal Vikings and were probably nasty bullies in normal life.

STEINTHOR'S STORY

One saga tells of how a skilled warrior called Steinthor saved his friend's life. During a battle Steinthor's friend was fighting on ice when he slipped and fell over. As an enemy warrior prepared to finish the friend off, Steinthor ran forward, held up his own shield over his friend to ward off the enemy blow, while with his other hand he slashed off the enemy's leg, and 'in one and the same moment' leapt in the air so that a blow aimed at him by another enemy warrior passed safely beneath his legs.

Vikings weren't bothered about death or dead bodies. There's an Irish description of a Viking victory feast after a battle in about 880: *the army encamped on the very battlefield to cook their food. The cauldrons were placed on top of heaps of fallen Norwegians, with spits stuck in among the bodies, and the fires burning them so that their bellies burst, revealing the welter of beef and pork eaten the night before.*

SPOT THE SPARE LIMB!

In this picture there's one limb more than there ought to be. Can you see which it is?

Fearsome Forts

There could be more to Viking military technique than a berserk charge by wild men in 'swine array'. Some Viking kings had standing armies. In Denmark there were four great military camps, all built to the same design. Each could house some five and a half thousand warriors. They were built late in the Viking Age after the days of small scale raiders were over.

As well as camps for their warriors, the Danish kings built defensive fortifications. The biggest was the Danevirke, a huge rampart which stretched for nearly fourteen kilometres across the bottom of Denmark.

The Danevirke had one opening - enough to let a road pass through it - in case the Danes wished to march south. After all, the Danes could raid south overland if they wanted to; all the other Vikings had no choice but to go by water ...

ROW, ROW, ROW, THE BOAT

A FIGHT ON THE OCEAN WAVE

Nowhere in Denmark is further than fifty-six kilometres from the ocean and Norway is narrow too. So the sea was on the Vikings' doorstep and they needed it like a joy-rider needs the open road. They learned to build ships as beautiful as swans, but a lot more dangerous.

On an average raid there might be up to sixty warships, or *longships* as they are known. The longships were fast and sleek. Under sail they could reach speeds of more than sixteen kilometres per hour, which is not bad for a wind-powered ship. They carried forty oarsmen or more. The *Long Serpent* of

King Olaf Trygvason, built in the winter of AD 999, had sixty-four oarsmen. These sailors were always free men, unlike the crews of slave-galleys in the Mediterranean Sea. The captain had to be careful how he treated them.

The very first boats in Scandinavia were made of leather stretched over a wooden frame, but these were to the Viking longship what a pedal-bike is to a high-powered motorbike. By 350 BC early versions of the longship, like the Hjortspring ship, were being built with most of the features of Viking-age ships.

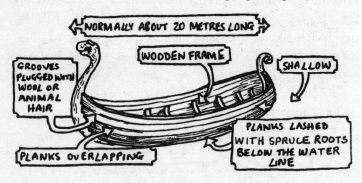

NORMALLY ABOUT 20 METRES LONG

WOODEN FRAME

SHALLOW

GROOVES PLUGGED WITH WOOL OR ANIMAL HAIR

PLANKS LASHED WITH SPRUCE ROOTS BELOW THE WATER LINE

PLANKS OVERLAPPING

The Hjortspring ship was *clinker-built* of overlapping planks. It had twenty oars but no sail; sails were added by the Vikings. The longships were shallow-bottomed, which meant that they could be drawn up silently on

SHSSSS!

any shelving beach and they could be sailed up shallow rivers to strike deep inland.

As well as using their ships for inland raids, it seems that the Vikings also used them for sea battles. In a sea battle the ships of a fleet might be lashed together to give a firm footing for the warriors, and some ships might have an iron frame lashed to the front end to act as a ram. Wooden screens were tied to the sides to fend off arrows.

Sea battles began with a storm of arrows and spears, then the ships crashed together and warriors sprang forward across the bows. The men in the bows did the hand-to-hand fighting; it was a mark of honour to be a 'stem-dweller', and row in the bows of the ship. Those at the back fired arrows over the heads of the fighters and waited to take the places of those who fell.

Knorr v. Longship Beauty Contest

Which do you prefer?

We know a lot about Viking ships, especially from the remains of three longships taken from Norwegian burial mounds: the Osberg, Gokstad and Tune ships. As well as longships, the Vikings

LONGSHIP

DETACHABLE FIGUREHEAD. IT WAS THOUGHT TO BE BAD LUCK TO LAND WITH IT ATTACHED.

SMALL DINGHY

20 METRES LONG

LEATHER BUCKET FOR BAILING

SEA-SICK VIKING

also built *knorrs*, or cargo-ships. Knorrs were shorter and stubbier than longships, with wide middle sections to hold cargo. They were very sea-worthy and useful. Vikings loved them. The greatest compliment that a Viking could pay to a beautiful woman was to call her 'knorr-breasted'.

KNORR

GILDED WEATHER VANE

SIDE TILLER

15 METRES LONG

CARGO HOLD

ROUNDED OR 'SWAN-BREASTED' AT THE FRONT.

A Night on the Ocean Wave

For all their skill as sailors the sea was still a very dangerous place for Vikings. We know of at least one knorr which was tossed right up in the air by the waves and landed bottom up.

On a dark night on the Atlantic Ocean, when the waves were high as a house, a longship wasn't a very comfortable place to be either. The warriors sat hunched on their sea-chests, their cloaks wrapped around them. They might hoist a long tent on the deck and snuggle down in two-man leather sleeping bags to snatch what sleep they could out of the spray and wind. But it was impossible to cook on board ship if they wanted a hot meal, so if they could, they preferred to pull in to the nearest shore at night and to pitch their tents on dry land.

So Long, Longships

For three hundred years longships ruled the sea-lanes of northern Europe. But eventually new ship-designs caught up with them. Other countries started to build ships higher out of the water. This meant that in a sea battle they could fight the Vikings from above, which was a big advantage in the days of spears and bows and arrows. The Vikings tried building fighting-platforms at the front and back of their ships, but their enemies just built platforms on their higher ships and kept the advantage of height. Finally, after several hundred years, the Viking longship ceased to rule the seas of Northern Europe.

GO WEST, YOUNG MAN

BUT FIRST, YOU HAVE TO KNOW THE WAY...

If you're rocking in a small boat in the middle of a vast ocean it's very hard to know where you are or which way to go. Despite this, and without any modern aids to navigation, the Vikings travelled all over the North Atlantic without great difficulty. Some of their directions for even the longest journeys seem amazingly casual:

THINGS VIKINGS DIDN'T HAVE

- Ship's compasses
- Radar
- Satellite positioning systems
- Sonar

THINGS VIKINGS DID HAVE

🔹 A knowledge of the sea

🔹 A bearing dial, for working out direction relevant to the sun or the North Star.

🔹 Luck

🔹 On overcast days they may have looked for the sun with a type of see-through stone which became cloudy when pointed towards the light.

Sometimes they got it wrong. In fact most of the great Viking discoveries were made by seamen who had been blown off course ...

THE FAROES AND BEYOND

Having attacked Ireland, mainland Britain and the Orkney Islands, the Vikings were ready for longer voyages far out of sight of land.

The Faroes are a bleak chain of islands which jut from the ocean like rotten teeth halfway between Scotland and Iceland. Some time around 820 a Viking called Grim Kamban visited them. He probably sailed there from Ireland, as his second name is an Irish nickname meaning *crooked*. The only people he found living on the Faroes were some Irish monks, known to the Vikings as *Papar*.

The Papars liked the Faroe Islands, describing with pleasure how in summer when the sun hardly set they could pick the lice from their shirts in the middle of the night. Papars were brave but they were dead unfriendly. Their custom had been to launch out to sea in tiny round leather-covered boats called *currachs* and let the wind and the waves take them. With luck they would bump into an empty island where they would build a tiny shed and live with just a few sheep for company - and strictly no other people nearby.

More Scandinavians soon followed Grim Kamban to the Faroes, and the Papars left. Nowadays the capital of the Faroes is called *Torshavn* - or *Thor's Haven*, after the Norse god *Thor*.

'Not a Nice Land - Iceland' (says Floki)

After the Faroes, the next step for the Vikings was Iceland, halfway to America - well almost. The first Viking to spot it was probably a Swede called Gadar who was blown there while sailing from the Hebrides to the Faroes in 880. Or it may have been a Viking

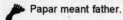 Papar meant father.

called Nadod who was blown off-course while sailing from Norway to the Faroes in 860. Either way, other Vikings soon followed.

THE TALE OF FLOKI AND THE RELUCTANT RAVENS

Iceland was called Iceland by the explorer, Floki, who was the first to try and settle there, but took a dislike to it. Floki took three sacred ravens with him when he set sail from the Faroes. He released the first raven once he was well out to sea but it flew straight back to land. Then having sailed a little further, he released the second - but it flew back to the ship. Finally he released the third raven and it flew straight ahead. He followed it - to Iceland.

Unfortunately Floki forgot to bring any hay with him so that his cows, sheep and horses died over winter. He and his crew had a terrible winter and left as soon as possible in the spring. He called the land Iceland in disgust, but it was his own fault that he couldn't stay there. He should have brought the right provisions with him.

Iceland was an empty country when Floki arrived, except for a few Papars who soon left. A flood of settlers followed him, bringing their families, slaves and followers with them. Four hundred leading men and three thousand of their families and followers are recorded in a book called the Landnamabok, in a detailed record of the first settlers.

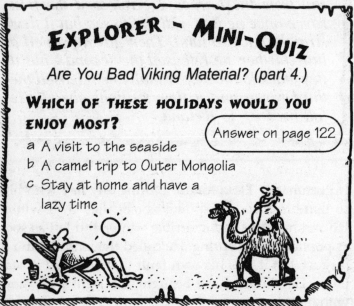

EXPLORER - MINI-QUIZ

Are You Bad Viking Material? (part 4.)

WHICH OF THESE HOLIDAYS WOULD YOU ENJOY MOST?

Answer on page 122

a A visit to the seaside
b A camel trip to Outer Mongolia
c Stay at home and have a lazy time

THE TALE OF ERIK AND THE NOT-SO GREENLAND

In 982 a red-haired man-killer called Erik the Red decided to check out the rumours of a new land in the west, told to him by a sailor called Gunnbjorn who had seen land while storm-driven fifty years before. Eric was eager to search for this new land because he had to leave Iceland in a hurry, having just killed someone. It was becoming a habit. The same thing had happened twice before, another killing in Iceland and one in Norway.

There may have been an attempt to settle on the east coast of Greenland in 978, but a savagely cold winter had put an end to it. Erik was the first proper settler. He decided to explore the west coast. For three years he sailed up and down, noting the best places to set up farms. When he returned to Iceland he called the new country 'Greenland' to make it sound attractive. By 986 he had persuaded twenty-five shiploads of land-hungry settlers to follow him to the new country.

The number of Norse people living on Greenland grew to over four thousand at its peak. They traded with Inuit, or Eskimos, in the far north and kept in contact with Iceland and Norway back home. Mainly they lived by farming; there were a hundred and ninety farms strung out along the west coast, rearing cattle, sheep and goats. The site of Erik's farm, *Bratahlith*, can still be seen. It is overgrown with grass and surrounded by the ruins of later farm buildings.

But a farming life wasn't enough for Erik's family. They needed something more ...

AMERICA!

Erik the Red's son, Leif Eriksson was called *Leif the Lucky*. He heard tell of a land to the west of Greenland from a Viking called Bjarni. In 986 Bjarni had set out from Iceland for Greenland and missed it in a fog, sighting a strange coast before turning back. Bjarni was probably the first European ever to see America, more than five hundred years before Columbus.

Around 1003 Leif bought Bjarni's ship ⏴ and they set sail together from the farm at Bratahlith. They saw

 He may have bought the ship in the belief that it would 'know the way', having been there before.

three new countries, which they called Slab Land, Forest Land and Wine Land (Vinland). Vinland was given its name because wild grapes grew there. It was where the Vikings

landed. It may have been New England. In the words of the Greenlanders' Saga:

They went ashore and looked about them. The weather was fine. There was dew on the grass, and the first thing they did was to get some of it on their hands and put it to their lips, and to them it seemed the sweetest thing they had ever tasted.

They found wild wheat, timber and grapes and lots of salmon and decided to stay the winter, sailing home to Greenland in the spring with a cargo of timber and dried grapes.

WE'VE COME TO STAY

Back home in Greenland, Leif got busy organising a bigger expedition, and after a few years he set out with a hundred and sixty people in three ships. Bjarni, the first European to sight America, was one of the party.

Things got off to a poor start when one of the leaders, Thorhall the Hunter (who was a bit mad) became really unpleasant and said that they were looking for Vinland in the wrong direction. He sailed off in one of the ships and eventually reached Ireland where he and his men were tortured and used as slaves by the Irish.

The Vikings who made it to Vinland stayed there only three years. They were plagued by quarrels over women and attacks by native Americans or Indians - *Skraeling* or *screechers* as the Vikings called them - who killed Leif's brother, Thorvald.

Bad trouble started after the second winter when a Skraeling was killed by a Viking while trying to steal some Viking weapons. The Skraelings sought revenge and attacked the Vikings with a large catapult handled by several men. It threw a dark-coloured ball and killed one man. The Vikings retreated, but were rallied by Erik the Red's daughter, Freydidis who grabbed the

dead man's sword. Two Vikings and four Skraelings were killed in the battle that followed. From then on the Vikings were always in danger from native Americans.

They decided to make a new camp on an island further north where they would be safer from the Skraelings. But they quarrelled endlessly over women and in the summer they decided to give up and go home. Bjarni, who had started it all, was drowned in the Irish sea trying to get back to Greenland.

 The Algonquin tribe of native Americans have a tradition that their ancestors had such a weapon. It threw a boulder sewn into a skin.

FORGOTTEN HEROES

For hundreds of years no one knew for sure that the Vikings had discovered America. It was just a story written in two ancient Icelandic sagas, the Greenlanders' Saga and Erik's Saga. Now there's no doubt:

 Clue no 1:
Remains of Viking longhouses found at L'Anse-aux-Meadows on Newfoundland.

 Clue no 2:
Indian arrowhead found in Greenland.

 Clue no 3:
A Viking coin found in New England.

ALL RIGHT THEN, GO EAST!

RAIDERS IN RIVER BOATS

While Norwegians raided and traded in the west, Swedes did the same in the east, and the Danes did a bit of both. There was a bit less raiding and a bit more trading in the east on the whole, but like all healthy Vikings, the Swedes and Danes could turn their hand to either as it suited them.

The eastern Vikings traded over huge distances. The small figure of a Buddha from far-away India has been

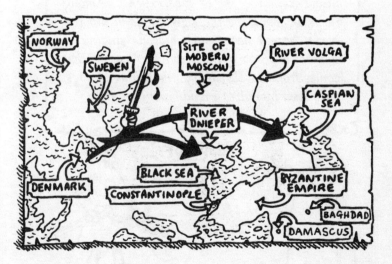

found in Sweden along with great glittering hoards of eastern coins and other goods. They traded with Arab countries and with the mighty Byzantine Empire. Wealth from the eastern trade flooded back into Denmark and Sweden in a great shiny river of gold and silver. Three large Viking towns called Ribe, Birka and Hedeby grew out of this trading wealth.

Hedeby was the largest town. It was at the Scandinavian end of several long trade routes to Arab lands far in the south, where slaves, amber, walrus ivory and furs were sold, and wine and other southern luxuries were bought. A visiting Arab called Ibrahim ibn Ahmed a'Tartushi left a description of Hedeby in the 950s. He thought the Vikings were savages:

A very large town beyond the furthest end of the ocean. When a child is born they often throw it in the sea to save expense. Among them women have the right to claim divorce. Never have I heard such hideous singing as that of the people of this town; it is a growl that comes from the throat like the baying of dogs, only even more like a wild beast than that.

WOOF!

But the people of Hedeby were more than savages. Most lived in small square houses which stood in rows on either side of wooden roads, each with its own well and fenced-in courtyard. Many were craftsmen making jewels, decorated weapons and ornaments from materials such as soapstone, glass, amber, silver and walrus ivory.

Vikings liked to smother the things they made in swirling, crawling patterns. There were many different styles. Here are some of them:

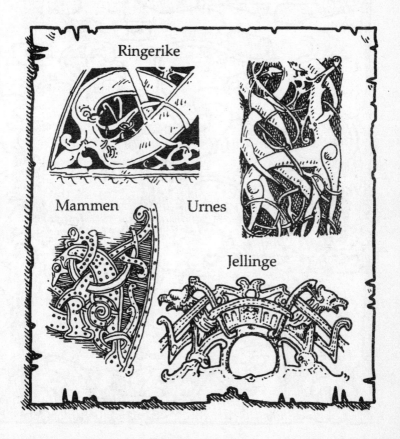

Ringerike

Mammen

Urnes

Jellinge

A-Mazing Gripping Beasts

The Viking Age started with the Gripping Beast style where strange animals or people clutch at each other and themselves with hands, feet and paws. Other styles used weaving winding lines like drawn-out knitting. This picture is made up from a bit of both.

Follow the line which ends at the bottom of page 83.

NEVER TRUST A RUS

From Denmark, and especially from Sweden, the Vikings set off across the huge wastes of western Russia in search of slaves and other goods. At that time Russia was the land of the wild Slavs (where the word slave comes from). The Slavs were the ancestors of modern Russians and other East-European peoples. They called the Vikings *Rus* ◄, which is where the name *Russia* comes from. The Rus built the Russian towns of Kiev, Smolensk and Novgorod and it was the Rus who founded the state of Russia, after the local Slavs asked a Viking called Rurik to rule for them.

HEAVE HO!

AWAY WE GO

When they had gathered their trade-goods, the Rus would travel south, by river whenever possible, assembling their fleet at a fortress just south of Kiev before setting off down the River Volga to the Black Sea.

Rus was possibly a Finnish word for a Swede before the Slavs got hold of it.

Once on the river they drifted downstream using local boats. When they came to rapids they would let most of the people walk, leaving their goods in the boats, while the boatmen plunged into the water naked,

steering the boats with poles. If the water was specially difficult they would carry both goods and boats overland until the water was calmer again.

Some Arabs travelled north in order to meet them half way and these Arabs left the earliest descriptions of the eastern Vikings. The Rus wore wide baggy eastern trousers and were very handsome and clean according to one Arab (although another describes them as repulsively dirty in their personal habits, so we're not completely sure). They kept lots of slave girls, sacrificed men, women and cattle to their gods, usually by hanging, and were quarrelsome. Sword or axe duels were common.

The eastern Vikings spread their net wide. They travelled far south and east into Muslim territory, destroying the Khazar town of Abasgun on the southern shore of the Caspian Sea around 864. But their favourite destination was Constantinople (now Istanbul), the capital of the Byzantine Empire ...

Constantinople, or *Mikligardr* (the Great City), as the Vikings called it, was on the southern tip of the Black Sea, and was the largest city in the world. It had half a million inhabitants. It was shiny with gold and had so many churches they were like molehills in a meadow. Constantinople drew the Rus like wasps to a jam-pot.

The Rus reached Constantinople by 838. By the 860s a Rus fleet had ravaged the towns along the shores of the Black Sea and appeared before the walls of the Great City, only to be defeated by a violent storm. In 907 they were back again - and again. But the Rus never captured Constantinople: the Byzantines were too crafty. They made a treaty with the Rus in 911-12 which covered things like murder, theft and shipwreck (there was already some sort of arrangement for free baths). The Rus were allowed to spend the summer in the suburbs of the city but they could not enter the city proper in groups of more than fifty men, and they had to be unarmed. After the treaty of 911-12 the Byzantines were able to deal fairly peacefully with the Rus - well, most of the time anyway.

THE TALE OF IGOR AND THE FLAME THROWERS

In 941, after thirty years of peace, a Rus chieftain called Igor attacked Constantinople with a large fleet. The Byzantines only had fifteen broken-down galleys to fight him with, but they were crafty as ever. They loaded their galleys with a chemical mixture called Greek Fire packed into wooden tubes cased in bronze. Then, the current being in the right direction, they let the galleys drift down on the Rus fleet. As the galleys closed the Byzantine crews squirted water at the bases of the wooden tubes. This had the effect of 'firing' them. Flames arched over the Rus ships. Thousands leapt into the water and those who reached the shore were slaughtered. The Rus kept the peace for some time after this defeat.

Rus were useful in the Byzantine Emperor's bodyguard, which was soon packed with large fair-haired men and became known as the *Varangian Guard*. Varangian was what the Byzantines called the Vikings. As Varangians the Vikings fought for Byzantium in the area of modern Iraq and even attacked Athens. If you want proof, there's a stone lion in Venice which was taken from Athens and has Viking graffiti on it.

There's another way of getting to the east from Scandinavia. Sail south down the coast of Europe, turn left at the Straits of Gibraltar and keep straight on down the Mediterranean Sea. Take a look at these cuttings from my scrap-book!

RAIDER'S DIGEST

The voice of Vikings everywhere
Circulation 2,000,000

SEVILLE SLAUGHTER 844

Viking raiders have attacked the Spanish city of Seville, ruled by the Moors of North Africa. The men of the city are said to have been killed, and the women and children taken captive. Regrettably, latest reports say the Vikings have been defeated by the Moors and have retreated to France.

LUNA LOSERS IN MASSACRE MIX-UP 860

Top Viking chiefs Bjorn and Hastein 🏴 have sacked the city of Luna in Italy mistaking it for the city of Rome because of its gleaming white walls. They tricked their way into the city by pretending to be refugees needing to bury their chief. Once inside the city, Hastein leapt from his coffin and led a splendid killing-feast in the narrow streets.

RAIDERS RETURN 862

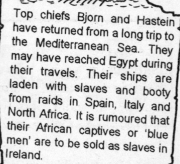

Top chiefs Bjorn and Hastein have returned from a long trip to the Mediterranean Sea. They may have reached Egypt during their travels. Their ships are laden with slaves and booty from raids in Spain, Italy and North Africa. It is rumoured that their African captives or 'blue men' are to be sold as slaves in Ireland.

THE BULLDOG BITES BACK

BRITAIN AT BATTLE-STATIONS – THE STORY SO FAR

1 Britain and Europe had been flattened by Viking raiders for over fifty years: raiders like Ragnar who attacked Paris in 845, withdrawing only after being offered seven thousand pounds of silver.

2 Society was breaking up under Viking attack. A monk wrote: any slave runs away from his master and, deserting Christianity, becomes a Viking.

3 Europe started to defend itself, building defensive bridges across rivers and fortifying towns.

4 In England the Saxon Kingdoms were weak and divided.

90

5 In 865 a 'Great Heathen Army'  looking for easier pickings landed in England from Europe. It was led by the sons of Ragnar, seeking vengeance for his execution by the Saxon king, Ella, in a snake-pit in York a few years before. As Ragnar said in the snake-pit: *the piglets would be grunting if they knew what was happening to the boar.*

THE SONS OF RAGNAR

IVAR THE BONELESS

HALFDAN

UBBI

6 In 866 the Viking army captured York and took revenge for the death of Ragnar by carving the *blood-eagle* on the back of King Ella. They cut his ribs from his spine, pulled out his lungs and spread them on his back so they looked like the wings of an eagle. It may have been a sacrifice to the Viking god, Odin.

7 For the next few years the Vikings rampaged almost unchecked around England and carved out a kingdom for themselves, know as *Danelaw*, based in York.

NORTHUMBRIA

DANELAW

MERCIA

WESSEX

 Armies at this date were actually very small. The Great Heathen Army was probably around five hundred men.

Meanwhile in 871 Alfred, England's greatest king ever (in fact the only one to be called *Great*), became king of the Saxon kingdom of Wessex at the young age of twenty-two or twenty-three. Wessex was so weak when Alfred came to the throne that in 875, when the Vikings mounted their usual rampage, he had to hide all summer in the Somerset marshes at Athelney.

FAMOUS CAKE STORY

While he was hiding in the Somerset marshes, Alfred did a lot of his planning for the reconquest of England. The story goes that once he hid in the hut of a peasant woman. She asked him to watch some cakes that she was cooking while she went out, but Alfred was so deep in thought that he burned the cakes. When she came back she told him off.

ALFRED'S PROBLEM

The Vikings could raid anywhere at any time. It was impossible to know where they would strike first and to have an army ready in the right place to fight them.

Alfred's people were Saxon farmers. They could not stay in the army all year; they had to look after their farms, and when they were busy farming they were easy prey for the Vikings.

ALFRED'S SOLUTION

Alfred and his successors built a network of fortified towns and strong-points, called *burghs*, all over his kingdom. The plan was that in case of Viking attack no one would be more than a day's walk away from somewhere safe, so most Burghs were about thirty kilometres apart. These burghs were the start of many English towns. If you live in a town ending in -burgh or -bury, then now you know how it started.

 **!** He created England's first navy, building ships to his own design. They were bigger than Viking ships, with sixty oars, and higher out of the water, which was better for sea battles.

He split his army in half. One lot stayed at home while the other half fought. That way there was always someone to fight and someone to do the farming.

 **!** In 886 the Saxon kingdom of Mercia accepted Alfred's leadership so that he controlled most of Saxon-held England.

! But fighting wasn't all that our hero was interested in. At that time most writing was in Latin, but Alfred wanted people to write in Anglo-Saxon as well, the language which modern English grew from. He asked his Welsh friend, Bishop Asser, to start the *Anglo-Saxon Chronicle*, which is how we know so much about the Viking raids on

England. On top of this, Alfred made all his top noblemen learn to read and write. No wonder he was called Great; he helped create a lot of our towns and our language.

WHEN IS A VIKING NOT A VIKING?

Since Alfred had made raiding difficult, the Vikings - or Danes as they were now known - decided to stay peacefully in their kingdom of Danelaw and its capital, York. The Danelaw was accepted by Alfred in a treaty with the leader of the Danes, Guthrum, in 878.

In fact by 878 most of the Danes in Danelaw weren't Viking raiders at all. They were just ordinary settlers. They even left the Saxons unharmed in their villages and cleared unused land to start their own farms. Villages and farms in what was once Danelaw still often have Danish names. Danes even copied Saxon farming methods, including the *open field system,* which is not farming based on leaving gates open, but a method of sharing huge fields.

Soon Danes and Saxons started mixing and their descendants all became English men and women. In fact modern English is based on the way people spoke in the East Midlands, where Danes and Saxons mixed most freely.

But if you think everyone lived happily ever after, think again ...

DISASTER STRIKES AGAIN!

ENGLAND - THE STORY SO FAR

1 878-899 King Alfred triumphed over the Danes in many battles.

2 After Alfred's death his successors bravely kept up the fight.

3 In 954 the last Viking king of York, Eric Bloodaxe was driven from his kingdom, although the Danish settlers were allowed to stay.

4 Then came more than twenty years of peace.

> Peace! - You'll be lucky. Take a look at these pages from *RAIDER'S DIGEST*!

RAIDER'S DIGEST

The voice of Vikings everywhere
Circulation 2,000,000

WE'RE BACK! 980

We are very pleased to announce the first successful Viking raid on England in more than twenty years. The town of Southampton has been sacked and most of its people killed or taken captive. Excellent work, Vikings!

LONDON'S BURNING! 982

Following resumption of raiding in 980 we are delighted to report that the city of London has been burned down following a raid for loot and slaves.

FINANCIAL PAGES
DOLE OUT THE DANEGELD! 991-1012

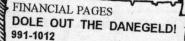

Overflowing treasure chests in Scandinavia may lead to inflation if raiding continues. Danegelds paid out by English kings have been getting bigger, rising from £10,000 in 991 to £48,000 in 1012. Someone should have told them - 'once you start paying the Danegeld, you never get rid of the Dane!'

MALDON MAYHEM 991

Viking hero Olaf Trygvasson has smashed a Saxon army at Maldon in Essex. The Saxons are said to have fought bravely but they were no match for our brave boys. A Saxon poem is now being written about the battle.

MASSACRE! 1002

All Danes living in England, men, women and children, have been massacred on the orders of Saxon king, Ethelred the Unready. It is said that the sister of King Svein Forkbeard of Denmark is among the victims.

ARCHBISHOP AXED 1011

Never let it be said that our brave boys are without mercy. Reports have just reached us of how newly-Christian Viking Thrum has helped the Archbishop of Canterbury to heaven. It seems that following the capture of Canterbury our boys found a store of wine and got very drunk. Understandably they became a little out of hand and started to pelt the Archbishop to death with bones and ox-heads. Thrum, seeing the archbishop's problem, put him out of his misery with an axe-blow to the head.

WHAT A LAF! OLAF! 1009

Viking king, Olaf Haraldsson, has torn down London Bridge by pulling at it with grappling irons attached to his ships. A song has been written about it. 'London Bridge is falling down, falling down, falling down'

FORKBEARD FIGHTS BACK 1013

Danish Viking king, Svein Forkbeard, having returned to England to take revenge for Ethelred's massacre, has completed the conquest of the country in time for Christmas. At last the whole country has fallen to the Vikings. Congratulations, comrades!

THE END GAME

Svein Forkbeard had succeeded in conquering England by Christmas 1013, but he didn't live long enough to enjoy it. He died in February 1014. After a bit more fighting his son, King Canute, took the throne and ruled over both England and Denmark.

CANUTE

Canute turned out to be quite a good king and England had twenty more years of peace.

FAMOUS CANUTE STORY

One day King Canute's chair was taken down to the coast. He sat down in it and ordered the tide to turn back. It didn't of course. It's said that his courtiers had persuaded him to do this out of flattery, to show that he was such an incredibly powerful king that even the sea obeyed him. Actually Canute wanted to show his courtiers that only God can control the tide - Canute was a Christian.

Canute died in 1035 and an English king, Edward the Confessor, soon took the throne of England. But other Vikings didn't give up without a struggle. Harald Hardrada 🐾 (means Hard Ruler, he was also known as Harald the Ruthless) prepared to attack in 1066. Harald was a ferocious Viking chief.

RUTHLESS HARALD AND THE BURNING BIRDS

At the age of eighteen Harald moved to Constantinople and joined the Byzantine Emperor's Varangian Guard, bringing with him a following of five hundred warriors. He fought for the Byzantines in Palestine and Sicily and was soon on the way to establishing his reputation for ruthlessness. One saga describes his cruel trick for taking a Sicilian town. He ordered birdcatchers to collect a number of small birds. Their wings were then smeared with sulphur and wax, and wood-shavings stuck to them. The shavings were then set alight and the birds released so that they flew back to their nests in the town and set light to the thatched roofs of the defenders' houses.

RUTHLESS HARALD AND THE GREAT ESCAPE

One of Harald's Byzantine employers was the Empress Zoe. She was as ruthless as Harald in her own way: she had her husband murdered in his bath, and her second husband became the new emperor. Perhaps distrusting Harald, Zoe accused him of stealing from the royal treasury and had him thrown in prison. Harald escaped and joined a revolution against the empress and her new husband. He caught the new emperor and gouged out his eyes.

By this time Constantinople was getting too dangerous, even for Harald Hardrada. He escaped by boat with a picked group of followers. But out in the narrow waters of the Bosphorus he found that his way was barred by chains slung across the water from bank to bank to stop him. Nothing daunted, Harald slipped his ship over the chains by ordering everyone first to the back of the boat so that it tipped up at the front, then making them all move to the front of the boat when it was halfway over the chain.

HARALD AND THE COATLESS ARMY

Safely back in Scandinavia, Harald became King of Norway. This was where he earned his nickname Hardrada, meaning hard ruler. But Norway wasn't enough for him. His greedy eye soon turned towards England. In 1066 he attacked England with a fleet of three hundred ships and an army of nine thousand men.

But Harald's luck had run out at last. It was September when he invaded England and the weather was still warm. His Vikings took off their leather coats and were marching unprotected when they were surprised by an English army at Stamford Bridge in Yorkshire. Despite the surprise, the Vikings fought bravely and for a while the English were held off by a huge Viking who held the bridge and killed forty men with his axe. Once this giant had been speared from below (by an Englishman in a paddle boat), the end was near. Harald was killed by an arrow in his throat and the Viking army was crushed. With Harald Hardrada's death, the Viking Age in England was finally over.

Or was it?...

WILLIAM TAKES OVER

In 1066, while Harald Hardrada's army invaded England from the north, England was also threatened by Normans from the south.

The Normans were Vikings who had settled in France more than a hundred years earlier after the French king, Charles the Simple, signed a treaty with a Viking called Rollo 🐾. In return for promising to obey the French king and for converting to Christianity, Rollo was made lord of most of the lands of what is now Normandy - the land of the Norsemen. The Vikings liked France so much that within a hundred years they had all turned into French-speaking 'Normans', marrying French people and also, no doubt, enjoying a glass of wine for breakfast.

IS MY CROISSANT READY?

In 1066 William, Duke of Normandy, who claimed to be the rightful heir to the throne of England, backed his claim with a massive invasion force, landing on the south coast.

The English army marched south from Stamford Bridge as fast as they could to meet the Normans, but by the time they reached the south coast they were exhausted. At the Battle of Hastings Harold Godwin, the English leader, was killed by an arrow in his eye and William, Duke of Normandy, descendant of the Vikings, won the battle and became William the Conqueror, first Norman king of England.

The Viking conquest of England was finally complete.

DRUNK FOR EVER!
- WELL NOT QUITE

GHASTLY GROVES FOR GLOOMY GODS

The Vikings were the last pagans in western Europe. Their religion was a horrible gloomy religion and offered absolutely no hope and comfort to believers. You had to be pretty brave to believe in it at all and many Vikings didn't.

> We know about pagan Viking religion from poems. In particular a collection of thirty-nine poems called the *Elder Edda*, first written down in 1225 in Iceland but actually much older.

Viking religion involved a lot of sacrifice, including human sacrifice. Sacrifices were made in sacred woods and groves of trees. At their great 'temple' at Uppsala in Sweden there was a festival every nine years where they sacrificed 'nine heads of every living thing that is male' over a period of nine days. The bodies were hung up in the grove. Human sacrifices might be:

 hurled from cliffs

Drowned in wells or bogs

GLUG

Hung

Let's find out what drove them to it ...

THE BEASTLY BEGINNING OF EVERYTHING

Vikings believed that the first living creature was a horrible giant called Ymir who lived on milk from a god-like cow called Authumbla. Ymir was killed by his grandsons, Odin and two brothers. They used his body to make the world:

PLANTS FROM THE HAIR

SKY FROM THE SKULL

MOUNTAINS FROM THE BONES

CLOUDS FROM THE BRAINS

SOIL FROM THE FLESH

OCEANS AND LAKES FROM THE BLOOD

THE WORLD ACCORDING TO VIKINGS

You may think that the world is a round ball of matter flying round the Sun. Vikings thought differently. They thought that the Earth was a flat disc surrounded by an ocean.

FOUR DWARFS HELD UP THE SKY.

THE LAND OF JOTUNHEIM, THE ABODE OF THE GIANTS, WAS BEYOND THE OCEAN.

THE EARTH WAS A FLAT DISC CIRCLED BY A GREAT OCEAN.

THE NORNS WERE FATES WHO DECIDED WHAT WOULD HAPPEN IN THE LIVES OF ALL CREATURES.

AN EAGLE WAS AT WAR WITH THE SERPENT IN THE ROOTS.

RATATOSK, A SQUIRREL, CAUSED TROUBLE BETWEEN THE EAGLE AND THE SERPENT.

YGGDRASIL, THE WORLD TREE, HELD UP THE UNIVERSE. ITS TRUNK WAS ROTTEN.

ASGARD, THE CITADEL OF THE GODS, PERCHED ON A CLIFF.

BIFROST, THE RAINBOW BRIDGE, CONNECTED ASGARD TO EARTH.

MIDGARD, THE LAND OF HUMANS, WAS CIRCLED BY A HIGH FENCE.

NIDHOGG, THE SERPENT, GNAWED AT THE ROOTS OF YGGDRASIL THE WORLD TREE.

THE WELL OF FATE

Odin and Life in Asgard

Odin was the favourite god of Viking warriors. The bravest slain in battle could expect to end up in his great hall, called Valholl, the hall of the slain - normally called *Valhalla* in English. It had six hundred and forty doorways and the rafters in its roof were spear shafts. There the dead warriors could feast all night and fight all day - until night came again and their wounds were magically healed so that they were ready for another bout of feasting.

Odin's maid-servants were called the *Valkyries* or Choosers of the Slain. In early stories they visited battlefields and ate the corpses of the dead; in later versions they carried fallen warriors off to Valhalla.

Odin himself was no saint. He often travelled in disguise with a grey beard, an old blue cloak and a wide-brimmed hat, riding, on his eight-legged horse, Sleipnir. Wherever he went he caused trouble, hoping to start new fights so that more warriors would be killed. He had many names:

OH DEAR, ODIN

Odin also sacrificed himself to himself by hanging on the Windswept Tree (probably Yggdrasil) seeking the wisdom of the dead.

Viking religion is perhaps the only one where everything gets destroyed in the end and the forces of evil triumph. Only people as tough as the Vikings could bear to believe in it. The end of the world according to the Vikings was called *Ragnarok*, meaning the Doom of the Gods.

THE HORRIBLE END OF EVERYTHING

The gods knew what was going to happen to them, even while they feasted in their palaces in Asgard. They knew that *Midgardsorm*, the World Serpent, lurked deep beneath the ocean and *Fenrir*, an evil wolf, lay bound in a cavern far away.

The gods knew that as the end drew near, things would start to go wrong for them. Odin's son, Baldur, would be killed by the treachery of an evil half-god called Loki, and from then on nothing would be able to stop the horrible fate which awaited them. The world would be frozen in a terrible winter called the *Fimbul Winter*. There would be earthquakes, the sun would go out, the dwarfs would cower in their rock-dwellings and the chains which bound the forces of evil would be smashed apart - and that would be just the beginning.

Next all Hel would break lose - literally. Fenrir the Wolf would break free from his chains and charge towards Asgard with jaws which stretched from heaven to earth. Midgardsorm the Serpent would lash in anger and the sea would flood over the land. The dead would cross the ocean from Hel, the underworld, in a boat made of dead men's nails.

Finally the giants would ride towards Asgard from the south and all the monsters of land and sea would join their army. *Bifrost*, the Rainbow Bridge, would break under their weight.

Summoned by the horn of Heimdall, the watchman, the gods would take up their weapons and prepare for battle. Odin would lead his band of fallen warriors against Fenrir the Wolf but would be eaten up, although his son would tear Fenrir's jaws apart in vengeance. The god Frey would be killed by the leader of the giants. Heimdall and Loki would kill each other. Thor would kill the serpent but would fall down dead from its poison.

In this battle to end all battles all the gods would be killed, the earth would burst into flame, then in a final horrific catastrophe the earth would sink hissing and sputtering into the sea and steam would cover the stars. It would be the end of everything.

Small wonder that the Vikings took to Christianity. At least it has a happy ending.

SIX FEET UNDER

Vikings seem to have been confused about what happened to them after they were dead - those that weren't chosen to go to Valhalla. On the one hand they thought that they would go to Hel, the underworld; on the other hand they might live on in the grave itself. Sometimes Hel-shoes were tied to a corpse's feet for the long walk to the underworld.

Hel was a misty cold place ruled over by a goddess,

also called Hel. She was not an attractive person: her rotting body was half black and half flesh-coloured. Her palace was called Sleetcold and her dinner plate was called Hunger.

Vikings might be buried with a horse or a boat to help them on the journey. Their graves were usually shaped like ships. The most spectacular of all Viking methods of dealing with the dead was to place the body on a ship and then burn it. This custom is still remembered in the festival of *Up Helly Aa* on the Orkneys, when a specially-built Viking longship is set on fire.

THE TALE OF ASMUND AND THE IRKSOME SLAVE

Whether they went to Hel or stayed on in the grave, it was good for the dead to be buried with some of their possessions so as to make their next life more comfortable. Sometimes a slave or favourite wife was popped into the grave to keep them company. One of the first settlers on Iceland, a man called Asmund, was buried with a boat and a slave. Some time later a passer-by heard Asmund's voice chanting from the grave, saying that he didn't care for the slave's company and would rather be on his own. The grave was opened and the slave removed, and from then on Asmund was silent.

CLOUD OF GLOOM

WHAT DO YOU BELIEVE IN?

Check it out - are you bad Viking material? (part 5)

I WHICH OF THESE IS RIGHT?

a The sky is held up by a large pink
  elephant called Linda.
b The sky is made of a
  ragged blue cloak.
c The sky is held up by
  four dwarfs.

2 WHICH OF THESE IS RIGHT?

a Giants help gods fight
  the forces of destruction.
b Giants are large and
  friendly but a bit stupid.
c Giants are evil.

Answers on page 122.

WHAT HAPPENED NEXT?

TURN CHRISTIAN - OR ELSE!

QUESTION:
What happens to Vikings if they turn into Christians?

ANSWER:
They stop being Vikings - eventually.

The first wild raiders of Lindisfarne Island in 793 thought Christians were softies who couldn't defend themselves. However, later Vikings saw that there was more to Christianity than an easy source of loot and slaves. They learned that Christianity was the fashionable religion of civilised Europe and that Christians thought that Vikings were a bunch of ignorant barbarians.

YOU PATHETIC IGNORANT BRUTE

!?

One by one Viking kings converted to Christianity. Some kings and leaders were paid to convert, some did it as part of a peace treaty with a Christian king, one or two even believed in it and some of them no doubt just couldn't bear to think about Ragnarok, the Doom of the Gods, any more.

As for ordinary Vikings, they mostly became Christian because they were told to by their kings. In Scandinavia, the man who started the process was Harald Bluetooth King of Denmark (died 986). Poppa, the missionary who converted him, is said to have proved the power of Christ by putting his hand in a white-hot iron glove. When Harald saw that Poppa's hand was not damaged he converted to Christianity.

The conversion process was continued in Norway, Iceland and Greenland by Olaf Trygvasson, the raider who had smashed the Saxons at the battle of Maldon in 991. Olaf was a tough Viking and he used tough Viking methods to turn people to Christianity, but he was a real softy compared to Olaf the Stout , later Saint Olaf, who finished the conversion of Norway. Saint Olaf maimed, blinded or executed all his subjects who refused to convert.

Being Christian took the fire out of the Vikings eventually. Pagan habits such as human sacrifice and raiding gradually died out. The Swedes were the last to convert, probably because their big pagan temple at Uppsala was tended by pagan priests. The priests resisted change so as to keep their jobs.

LAST GASPS

The Viking Age died slowly. Their style of life lingered on in Scandinavia and the Scottish islands, and above all in Iceland, for a long time after it had died out in the rest of Britain and Europe. But the days of the

Vikings were numbered. They were too bold, too bad and too ready to learn new ways to stay Vikings.

The most far-flung Viking outpost of all never had a chance. Greenland was taken over by medieval Norway in 1261. Then as the climate grew colder, Inuit, or Eskimos, moved south and there were violent battles. Contact with Europe gradually died out. All the Viking settlers were dead by 1500 . When a ship reached Greenland in 1540, the sailors found only deserted farms.

As for their amazing discovery of America, descendants of the Greenland Vikings were still sailing to Vinland for timber as late as 1347, but eventually the contact was lost - and the memory with it.

 Evidence from graves shows that the last Greenlanders were 10 cm shorter on average due to bad diet caused by lack of sunshine to grow vegetables.

YEARS OF FEAR

A HANDFUL OF DATES

RANDOM RAIDS

793	Lindisfarne monastery attacked.
795	First Viking attacks on Ireland and Scotland.
799	Emperor Charlemagne organises defence against Viking raids on Europe.
814	Charlemagne dies. Europe is divided.
825	Vikings settle in the Faroe Islands.

THEY CAME TO STAY

839	Vikings spend winter in Ireland for the first time.
841	Dublin founded as Viking base.
844	First Viking attack on Spain.
850	Vikings pass the winter in England for the first time.
859-62	Bjorn Ironsides and Hastein raid Mediterranean.
860	First Rus attack on Constantinople.
865	'Great Heathen Army' invades England.
867	Danes capture York.
870-973	Vikings settle in Iceland.

BRITAIN BITES BACK

871-99	Alfred is King of England.
878	Danelaw established, Treaty of Wedmore.

885-86	Siege of Paris.
911	Rollo becomes first Duke of Normandy.
954	End of Viking Kingdom of York, Erik Bloodaxe killed.

DISASTER STRIKES AGAIN

980	Vikings start raiding England again. Varangian guard started in Constantinople.
986	Start of settlement of Greenland.
1016-35	Canute is King of England.
1042	Danish rule in England ends.
1043	Rus attack Constantinople for the last time.

THE END

1066	Harald Hardrada killed at Stamford Bridge. William the Conqueror wins Battle of Hastings.
1347	Greenlanders still sailing to Vinland.
1380	Inuit, or Eskimos, occupy last Viking settlements on Greenland.

ARE YOU BAD VIKING MATERIAL - ANSWERS.

Score 10 points for each right answer.

Part 1.	Part 2.	Part 3.	Part 4.	Part 5.
1. b	1. b	a or b.	1. c	1. c
2. c	2. b		2. a	2. c
3. b	3. c			

Less than 40	Hopeless - you probably faint at the sight of blood.
40+	Promising - for a wimp.
70+	Excellent - go out and buy an axe.

VILLAINOUS VIKINGS HALL OF FAME

❦ EGIL SKALLAGRIMSSON

The greatest of all the Viking poets and a great warrior, Egil made his first killing at the age of seven when he struck an eleven-year-old playmate. He was ugly (his nickname means 'bald'), dark, strong and sullen. He saved himself from death at the hands of *Erik Bloodaxe* by composing a poem in Erik's honour in Erik's hall at York.

❦ ERIK BLOODAXE

A ferocious Viking warrior, the son of *Harald Fairhair*, Erik was King of Norway for a short time from 930, and twice King of York between 948 and 954. He died in an ambush at Stainmore in England in 954.

😈 HARALD BLUETOOTH

King Harald built the large fortresses in Denmark and converted the country to Christianity. He was fatally wounded in a battle with his own son in 987 and fled the country, dying a few days later.

😈 HARALD FAIRHAIR

Harald's father drowned when he was ten and Harald fought his way to the top, founding the Kingdom of Norway shortly before 900. He had up to twenty sons including *Erik Bloodaxe* and Hakon the Good. He was succeeded by Erik Bloodaxe.

😈 HARALD HARDRADA

Perhaps the fiercest Viking of all, Harald fought his first battle in 1030 at the tender age of fifteen, fighting for his relative, King *Olaf the Stout* of Norway. The leader of the opposing army was Svein Forkbeard, son of Canute. Olaf died during the battle and Harald was wounded.

😈 HASTEIN

Hastein was known as a master of tricks and was a fearsome freelance raider. The raid round the Mediterranean in 859-62 with Bjorn Ironsides was his most famous adventure. He also led a raid of eighty ships up the Thames in 891.

😈 OLAF TRYGVASSON

Olaf was enslaved by pirates when only a child. Spotted by a fellow Swede, he was ransomed and taken to Novgorod where he recognised one of the slavers and killed him with a handaxe. A grandson of

Harald Fairhair, he became King of Norway in 995, converting to Christianity around the same time. He then terrorised his kingdom into converting as well. Died at the Battle of Svold in 1000.

🎸 OLAF THE STOUT

Ruled Norway 1016-28, when he was forced to leave the country following his brutal treatment of Norwegian pagans. He returned to Norway with an army of two thousand warriors in 1030 but was slashed to death with spear, sword and axe at the battle of Stiklarstadir, where his young relative, *Harald Hardrada*, was wounded. After his death Olaf the Stout became Saint Olaf.

🎸 ROLLO

Before he was made Duke of Normandy in 911 Rollo had been raiding in France for several years. In 912 he converted to Christianity and settled down to rule his new dukedom. Rollo may have been the same person as a Viking called *Hrolf the Ganger* or *Walker*, so-called because he was so big no horse could carry him.

INDEX